The Adventures of Huckleberry Finn

Mark Twain

D0920313

Level 3

Retold by John Votaw

Series Editors: Andy Hopkins and Jocelyn Potter

Pearson Education Limited
Edinburgh Gate, Harlow,
Essex CM20 2JE, England
and Associated Companies throughout the world.

ISBN: 9781447967507
First published 1884
Published by Puffin Books 1953
First Penguin Readers edition published 2000
This edition published 2008

1 3 5 7 9 10 8 6 4 2

Text copyright © Penguin Books Ltd 2000
This edition copyright © Pearson Education Ltd 2008
Illustrations by José Luis Navarro García
The author has asserted his moral right in accordance with the
Copyright Designs and Patents Act 1988

Set in 11/13pt A. Garamond
Printed in China
SWTC/01

Produced for the Publishers by AC Estudio Editorial S.L.

Published by Pearson Education Ltd

Acknowledgements
We are grateful to the following for permission to reproduce photographs:
World Pictures / Photoshot Holdings: Wojtek Buss page 76
Picture Research by Sandra Hilsdon

*Every effort has been made to trace the copyright holders and we apologise in advance for any unintentional omissions.
We would be pleased to insert the appropriate acknowledgement in any subsequent edition of this publication.*

Contents

1.1 What's the book about?

Look at the picture and discuss these questions. What do you think?

1 When and where does this story happen?

2 What can you tell about the people in the picture?

3 What kind of story will this be?

1.2 What happens first?

Read the title of Chapter 1 and the words in *italics* below it. Then look at the picture on page 4. What do you think it shows? Check (✓) the one correct statement.

1 ☐ It shows Huckleberry Finn's gang.

2 ☐ The boys are dangerous.

3 ☐ They steal from people.

4 ☐ They meet in the house of one of the boys.

5 ☐ Their families know where they are.

6 ☐ Boys soon leave the gang.

The Tom Sawyer Gang

"You can go home now," Tom told us. "We'll meet next week.
Then we can rob somebody and kill some people."

You don't know me if you haven't read *The Adventures of Tom Sawyer*. Mr. Mark Twain wrote that book, and most of it was true. Some things weren't exactly true, but everybody lies sometimes. Maybe not Tom's Aunt Polly or the **Widow** Douglas, though. They were in that other book.

The book ended like this. Tom and I found some money in a **cave** and it made us rich. We got $6,000 each—in gold! That's a lot of money. So we gave it to Judge Thatcher to keep it safe.

The Widow Douglas made me her son. "I'll teach you to be polite," she said. But I didn't want to be polite. I didn't like living in a house all the time. She even dressed me in nice clothes, but I really didn't like them. So one night I put on my old clothes and ran away.

But Tom Sawyer found me. He said, "I'm going to start a gang of robbers. If you go live with the Widow again, you can join the gang."

So I went back.

When I got home, the Widow cried with happiness. She kissed me and said, "My poor lost baby has come home." I didn't like that, but she meant it in a nice way.

Then it all started again. I had to sleep in a bed and I had to wear new clothes. I even had to be polite at dinner.

One night, I went to my room, feeling really lonely. Then I heard something. It sounded like a cat: "Me-yow, me-yow." I went to the window and looked down. It was Tom, waiting for me.

I climbed out the window to meet him. We went toward the trees in the Widow's backyard. We had to be very quiet. But when we passed the kitchen, I fell. The Widow's old **slave** Jim heard the noise and said: "Who's that?"

He listened carefully, but we didn't say anything. Then he came out into the backyard. He stood very near us. But we were very quiet, so he never saw us.

Then my foot began to itch, but I couldn't move—I didn't want him to hear me. The **itch** moved to my ear. Next, it moved to my back, right between

---

widow /ˈwɪdoʊ/ (n) a woman whose husband has died
cave /keɪv/ (n) a large natural hole in the side of a hill or under the ground
slave /sleɪv/ (n) someone who is owned by another person. A *slave* must work for that person without pay.
itch /ɪtʃ/ (v/n) to have an uncomfortable feeling on your skin so you can't stop touching it

my shoulders. This happens a lot. When I have to be quiet, I start to itch in a thousand places.

Soon Jim said, "Hey, where are you? Who's there? I know I heard something. I'm going to sit right here until you come out."

And he sat down between me and Tom, but still he didn't see us. He sat against a tree and waited.

My nose began to itch. Then I started to itch on the inside! I itched in eleven different places now. But then Jim fell asleep, and all my itches stopped.

Tom came to me very quietly. "Let's tie Jim to the tree, just for fun," he said.

"That's too dangerous," I said.

So then Tom went to Jim really carefully. He didn't want Jim to wake up. He took Jim's hat and hung it in the tree above his head. Then Tom and I ran as fast as we could into the woods.

The next day, Jim told everybody the story. "**Ghost**s put me to sleep," he said. "They picked me up and took me all over the state of Missouri. And then they brought me back, and hung my hat in the tree."

Later, when he told the story again, "all over the state of Missouri" changed to "all over the USA." The next time, it was "all over the world." Jim loved to tell stories, and people loved to hear them, too. Black people walked for miles to hear his story of the ghosts.

When we left Jim, he was still asleep. We ran all the way to town and found some other boys. Then we all followed Tom to his secret hiding place. There was a small hole in a hill and we climbed through, into a big cave. Tom told everybody about his gang of robbers. "We'll call it Tom Sawyer's Gang," he said, "and this will be our hiding place."

ghost /gəʊst/ (n) a dead person who has returned to this world

3

We all had to sign our names in blood. We also promised not to tell anybody about the gang.

Tom said, "If anybody tells, the gang will kill his family."

"Then Huck can't join because he doesn't have a family," somebody said.

"You can kill the Widow. She's almost my family," I suggested.

Everybody thought that was a good idea. So I joined the gang.

Then somebody asked, "What do robbers do?"

Tom said, "They steal things, of course. And they **ransom** people."

"Ransom? What does that mean?"

"I don't know," said Tom. "But robbers do it—I read it in a book. So we've got to do it. We have to bring prisoners to the cave and ransom them. Then we kill the men. But we keep the women until they fall in love with us."

I said, "Soon we'll have a cave full of women. There won't be any room for us robbers."

But we all agreed to be robbers.

"You can go home now," Tom told us. "We'll meet next week. Then we can rob somebody and kill some people."

So we all went home.

I climbed in my bedroom window just before the sun came up. My new clothes were all dirty but I was very tired. I couldn't worry about that.

ransom /ˈrænsəm/ (v) to keep someone prisoner until money is paid

CHAPTER 2

Pap Comes to Town

I thought, "If Pap's here, I'm in trouble. He probably wants my gold."
So I ran to the Judge's house.

The next morning, the Widow Douglas was very angry at me because of my dirty clothes. So I decided to be good.

I went out with the Tom Sawyer Gang for about a month, but we never robbed anybody and we never killed anybody. We only played. After a time I stopped going to the meetings. The other boys stopped going, too.

◆

Three or four months went past and it was winter time. The Widow sent me to school every day. I could spell and read and write a little. They wanted to teach me numbers, but I didn't like them and I didn't learn very much.

At first I hated school, but after that it was OK. When I got really bored with it, I didn't go. The teacher hit me the next day, but I didn't mind. Soon I even liked living with the Widow. Sometimes I still slept in the woods, but most of the time I liked sleeping in a bed.

I didn't know where Pap was. Pap's my dad. He came to town sometimes. I always hid in the woods when he came to town. One day, I heard that he was dead. But you could never be sure about Pap.

One morning, I was going to school. When I saw some footprints in the snow in front of the house, I looked closely at them. There was a small cross on the left foot. That was Pap's shoe! The cross was there because it kept away bad luck.

I thought, "If Pap's here, I'm in trouble. He probably wants my gold."

So I ran to the Judge's house.

"Do you still have my $6,000 of gold?" I asked.

"I do," he answered. "Do you want it?"

"No, sir!" I said. "I don't want it! I want *you* to have it. I want to give it to you!"

The Judge looked surprised. I said, "Don't ask me any questions about it. You just keep the gold."

He thought about this for a minute. He didn't know Pap was in town. But he was a smart man and he understood. "I'll buy your gold from you," he said. "I'll give you one dollar for it."

I agreed, and I signed a piece of paper. He gave me my dollar and I left.

That night, I went to bed early. When I opened my bedroom door, there was Pap! He was sitting on my bed.

Pap was almost fifty years old. He had long, dirty black hair. His face was white—like a ghost. But he wasn't dead. He looked at me and said, "You think you're a big man now, boy. And people say you can read and write, too." I didn't say anything. Then he said, "I can't read or write. Your mother couldn't read or write. So why do you need it?"

"I have to go to school," I told him. "The Widow sends me."

But he was angry and didn't want to listen to me. He asked me about my gold.

"I don't have any gold," I said. "I sold it to the Judge for a dollar."

Then he got really angry. "I'll talk to the Judge in the morning," he said. He took my dollar and left.

◆

Things were OK after that. I didn't see Pap again until the spring. Then he took me away from the Widow. He took me three miles up the river in a boat.

On the other side of the river, he had a **cabin**. He kept me there and I couldn't leave. Before bed, he always locked the door and put the key under his head.

"I don't want you to run away in the night," he said.

Sometimes he went away, but he always locked the door. He had a gun, too, and he kept it near him. So there was nothing that I could do.

I lived in the cabin with Pap for two months and I started to like it there. I didn't have to go to school, so I went **hunt**ing and fishing and swimming.

But sometimes Pap got angry and hit me. I didn't like that. Then he started hitting me all the time. Sometimes he went away and locked me in the cabin for two or three days. Then I got really lonely. So I decided that I had to escape.

cabin /ˈkæbɪn/ (n) a small house made of wood, usually in the forest or mountains

hunt /hʌnt/ (v) to follow and kill animals for food or sport

7

I tried everything, but I couldn't get out of the cabin. I couldn't get through the small window and I couldn't break the door. I looked everywhere for a way out.

Then one day, when Pap was in town, I found an old knife in the roof. Pap didn't know it was there. So I went under the bed and I started to cut a hole in the wall. It took a long time. I was almost finished when I heard a gun shot in the woods. It was Pap's gun! He was coming home. I stopped, hid my knife and waited.

Pap sent me to the river to catch some fish for dinner. I could see that the water was getting higher. This always happened in the spring and it was always fun. Things fell in the river. You could keep anything that you found. Sometimes I found big pieces of wood and I sold them to a man in town.

That day I was lucky. I looked up the river and saw a **canoe**. I jumped in the river and swam over to it. There was nobody in it, so I got in. I **paddle**d back to the riverside and hid it in the trees.

The next day, Pap went to town again, so I finished cutting the hole in the wall. Now I could escape! I didn't want him to follow me. So I broke down the door of the cabin from outside. Then I went into the woods and found a wild pig. I caught it and killed it with my knife. I took the pig back to the cabin and put its blood on the ground. There was blood everywhere. I put the pig in a big bag with some rocks. Then I pulled the bag to the river. There was blood from the cabin to the river. When I threw the bag into the river, it went all the way down to the bottom.

"Everybody will think I was killed by robbers," I thought happily. "And they threw me in the river."

Then I put some food in my canoe and paddled away.

canoe /kəˈnuː/ (n) a light, narrow boat which is pointed at both ends
paddle /ˈpædl/ (v) a short stick with a wide, flat end for moving a boat through water

2.1 Were you right?

Look back at your answers to Activity 1.2 on page iv. Then read these sentences. Are they true (T) or not true (NT)?

1   The gang meets in a cave.   ....

2   They steal gold.   ....

3   The gang is secret.   ....

4   They kill people.   ....

5   Tom Sawyer makes the gang's rules.   ....

6   Huck doesn't stay with the gang for long.   ....

2.2 What more did you learn?

1   **Answer these questions. Why:**

    a   does Huck have $6,000 in gold?

    ....

    b   does Huck live with the Widow Douglas?

    ....

    c   does Jim think that ghosts carried him away?

    ....

    d   does the Judge agree to buy Huck's gold for $1?

    ....

    e   does Pap lock Huck in his cabin in the woods?

    ....

    f   does Huck kill a wild pig?

    ....

2   **How is Huck's life different with Pap than with the Widow? Make notes.**

Life with the Widow	Life with Pap
goes to school	

2.3 Language in use

Look at the sentences on the right. Then find the correct endings to the sentences below.

> I climbed out the window **to meet** him.
>
> Black people walked for miles **to hear** his story.

1 Tom and Huck gave their gold to the Judge ...
2 Tom put the hat on a tree ...
3 The boys signed their names in blood ...
4 Huck went to school ...
5 Huck cut a hole in the cabin wall ...
6 Huck put pig's blood everywhere ...

to escape from Pap.
to please the Widow.
to trick Jim.
to trick Pap.
to join Tom's gang.
to keep it safe.

2.4 What happens next?

Read the words in *italics* on page 12. Then check (✓) the right answers. What do you think?

1 Who is speaking?

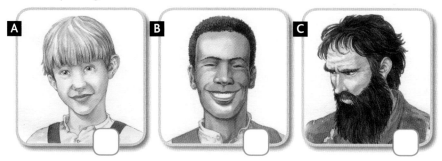

A   B   C

2 Who is the speaker talking to?

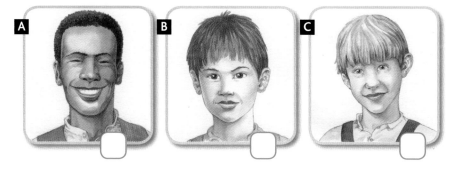

A   B   C

CHAPTER 3

On the River

*He said, "Please don't hurt me! I never hurt a ghost.
I always liked dead people and I was always your friend."*

I paddled for about five miles and then I was tired. I stopped on Jackson's Island, hid the canoe in some trees and went to sleep.

I woke up when I heard a "Boom!" It came from somewhere up the river. Then another "BOOM!" It was getting louder.

Then I saw the white smoke. They were shooting a big gun from a **steamboat** into the water because they wanted to find my dead body. They wanted it to come up to the top of the water.

I hid in the tall grass when the steamboat came near the island. I could see Tom Sawyer, Tom's Aunt Polly, the Widow Douglas, Judge Thatcher. Even Pap was there. Everybody was talking about me. They all thought I was dead. They shot the big gun again: "KABOOM!!" That one was really loud. It made my ears ring. But I didn't move from the tall grass. Then the boat went away.

I made a tent on the island and started to enjoy myself. In the daytime I went fishing and slept. I found a lot of fruit. I was the king of the island.

On the fourth day, when I was looking around, I stepped on a fire. It was still smoking. I didn't wait to see who made it. I just ran. I ran all the way back to my canoe. I thought I heard somebody. So I climbed a tree and looked around. But there wasn't anybody there.

That night, I went very quietly back to the fire. When I got there, I saw a man sleeping near it. He had a coat over his head. Then suddenly, he started to move and he took the coat off his face. It was Jim!

I was very glad to see him, so I said, "Hello, Jim!"

Jim jumped to his feet and his eyes opened wide with surprise. Then he fell down on his knees.

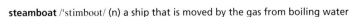

steamboat /ˈstimboʊt/ (n) a ship that is moved by the gas from boiling water

He said, "Please don't hurt me! I never hurt a ghost. I always liked dead people and I was always your friend."

"I'm not a ghost," I said, "and I'm not really dead."

Jim and I sat and talked. It was good to talk to somebody. Now I didn't feel so lonely.

"I left the Widow's house the day after you were killed," Jim told me. "I've been here on the island. I eat the fruit—there's no real food here."

It was almost morning, so I got my food out of the canoe. Then we made a fire and cooked breakfast. We had coffee and some fresh fish. Jim was the happiest man in the world.

After breakfast, Jim asked, "Huck, if you're still alive, then who died in the cabin?"

So I told him the story of my escape. "Why are *you* here?" I asked him.

He looked worried. "I can't tell," he said.

"Why, Jim?"

"You won't tell anyone, will you, Huck?"

"I won't, Jim," I promised.

"I believe you, Huck. I-I ran away."

That was very serious. It's illegal for a slave to run away. I didn't like runaway slaves. But I liked old Jim. I've known him all my life.

"I heard the Widow talking one night," he said. "She wanted to sell me for $800. I didn't want that—and I don't want to be a slave. So I ran away. I swam across the river. I want to be a rich man. See, Huck," he continued, "I have hairy arms. That means I'm going to be rich some day. Maybe I'm already rich. The Widow planned to sell me for $800. Now I own myself, so I own $800."

CHAPTER 4

The House in the River

Jim went to look at him. "He's not sleeping," Jim said, "he's dead!
Someone shot him in the back."

That same day, we walked around the island. At the top of a big hill, we found a cave.

"Let's hide all our things in the cave," Jim said. "We can sleep there, too."

It was a good idea, because that night it began to rain. It rained for ten days. The river got higher and higher, and the island almost disappeared. But we were dry in our cave and we still had plenty of food.

Early one morning, we saw a big house coming down the river. So we got in the canoe and paddled out to it.

We looked in the window. The house still had all its furniture. There was a bed, a table and two old chairs. A lot of clothes were hanging on the wall. There was something lying on the floor too. It looked like a man.

Jim said "Hello!" but the man didn't move. We thought he was asleep. Jim went to look at him. "He's not sleeping," Jim said, "he's dead! Someone shot him in the back. You can come in, but don't look at the dead man. It'll scare you."

He put an old shirt over the man's face and I went in.

In the house we found a lot of good things. When we left, we took knives, a bed sheet, some fishing line and clothes.

When we got in the canoe, Jim lay down under the bed sheet. He had to hide because he didn't want anyone to see him. Then I paddled back to the island. We got home safely.

One night, we caught part of a **raft**. It was made from pieces of wood that were tied together.

Two days passed, and the river went down again. Then we took our new fishing line and went fishing. The line was very strong, so we tied a dead **rat** on it. We soon caught a fish as big as a man. It was six feet long and it weighed more than two hundred pounds! We couldn't pull it in. We left it in the water until it got tired. Then it was easy. I'm sure it was the biggest fish in the Mississippi.

"I never saw a bigger one," Jim agreed. "We can take it to town and get a lot of money for it."

But we didn't take it to town—we ate it. It was really good.

The next morning, I felt bored. I looked through the clothes from the house

raft /ræft/ (n) long pieces of wood tied together into a kind of flat boat
rat /ræt/ (n) a small, wild, usually brown animal with a long tail that destroys food

15

and found eight dollars in an old coat. I wanted to go into town with the money for some excitement.

"Be careful," Jim said. "Everyone in town knows you. They think you're dead. Why don't you take those old clothes and dress like a girl? Nobody'll know you if you look like a girl."

I found a dress that was my size, and a girl's hat. I put them on. Then I practiced walking and talking like a girl.

"You look really good," Jim said. "But you don't walk like a girl."

So I practiced some more and got better. Just after dark, I got in the canoe and paddled across the river. Then I walked toward town.

CHAPTER 5

Huck Dresses Like a Girl

I was really scared and I started to shake. I didn't know what to do.
I said, "Please don't laugh at a poor girl like me."

Before I got to town, I saw a small house. I looked in the window and saw a woman at the kitchen table. She was about forty years old. I knew almost everyone in this town, but I didn't remember her. This was good luck.

I knocked on the door. I told myself, "I must remember that I'm a girl."

The woman opened the door. "Come in," she said. "Please sit down. What's your name?"

"Sarah Williams," I said.

"Where are you from?"

I told her, "I'm from Hookerville, about seven miles down river. My mother's sick. I've come here to see my uncle. He'll give me some money and then I can buy some medicine for my mother. My uncle's name is Abner Moore. Do you know him? He lives on the other side of town."

"No, I don't know him," she answered. "I'm new in town and I don't know many people."

I already knew that.

Then she said, "It's a long way to the other side of town. I think you should stay here tonight. Why don't you take off your hat?"

"No, I can't stay," I said quickly. "I'll rest for a short time, but then I must go."

"You can't go alone," she said. "My husband will be back soon. He can take you to your uncle's house."

Then she started talking about her family and her husband. She talked about Tom Sawyer and me, and the $6,000. She talked about Pap. He went to the judge, she said. He wanted the $6,000. Then she talked about Huck Finn's murder.

So I said, "Who killed him? We've heard this story down in Hookerville. But we don't know who killed Huck Finn."

"Some people say it was the Widow Douglas's slave, Jim," she said. "He ran away the day that Huck was killed. There's a $300 **reward** if you find him. But many people think it was Huck's father. They say he wanted Huck's money. A lot of people want to kill him. There's a $200 reward if you find him. But nobody knows where he is now."

---

reward /rɪˈwɔrd/ (n) money that is given for information or other help

"That's very interesting," I said. "So have people stopped looking for the slave?"

"No, not at all," she said. "They'll find him soon. Then we'll know what happened. Some people think the slave isn't far away. I think he's over on Jackson's Island. My husband's going there tonight with some other men."

Suddenly, I was very nervous. "Why don't they go in the daytime?" I said. "They can see better then."

"That's true," she said, "but the slave can see better, too."

"Oh," I said, "I didn't think of that."

She looked at me for a minute. Then she said, "Are you sure you don't want to take off your hat?"

"No, I'm comfortable with it on," I said.

Then she said, "What's your name again?"

"M-Mary Williams," I said. But that didn't seem right. So I didn't look at her when I answered.

"Didn't you say it was Sarah?"

"That's right," I said, "Sarah Mary Williams. Sarah's my first name. Some people call me Sarah. Some people call me Mary."

I felt better then, but I wanted to leave.

The woman started talking again. She told me about the rats in her house. They came out to look for food. She said, "When I see them, I throw things at them."

She had some heavy pieces of metal on the table. She picked one up and threw it at a rat in the corner. It hit the wall two feet away from the rat.

"It hurts my arm when I throw things," she said. "Can you throw something at the next rat?"

A few minutes later, the same rat came back. I picked up the piece of metal and threw it at the rat. I threw it hard and fast. But the rat moved too fast and I missed it.

The woman asked me to hold some wool for her. So I put out both my hands and took it. Then she said, "Watch for rats. Here, take this piece of metal."

She threw the metal at me. My hands were full, so I couldn't catch it with my hands. I put my legs together and caught it in my dress.

Then the woman looked straight at me and said, "Now, what's your real name?"

"Ex-Excuse me?" I said.

"What's your real name? Is it Bill, or Tom, or Bob?"

I was really scared and I started to shake. I didn't know what to do. I said, "Please don't laugh at a poor girl like me."

"Don't worry," she said, "I'm not going to hurt you and I won't tell anybody about you. You can believe me. Have you run away from home? Tell me. Maybe I can help."

So I started to tell another story. "I ran away from home," I said, "and I'm looking for my uncle. He'll look after me. That's why I came here to Goshen."

"Goshen, child?" she said. "This is St. Petersburg! Goshen's ten miles up the river."

"Oh! I've got to get to my uncle's house tonight. I have to go now," I said. I was happy with my story, and I really wanted to leave.

She gave me some food to take with me. And before I left, she said, "Now be careful. Don't talk to any women when you're dressed like that. They'll know you're a boy. And learn to act like a girl. Girls don't put their legs together when they catch things. And they don't throw things fast. They throw slowly, and they use every part of their body. You only used your arm. I knew you were a boy from the beginning. But I tested you because I wanted to be sure."

I thanked her for the food and left. I went straight to the river and I found my canoe. Then I paddled back to the island as fast as I could.

When I got there, Jim was asleep. I said, "Get up! We have to go!"

Jim didn't ask any questions. I didn't tell him about the men, but he knew.

We put all our things on the raft, and then we got in the canoe. We left the island very quietly and went down river.

3.1 Were you right?

Look back at Activity 2.4. Then write the correct names below.
Who:

1   are the people on the steamboat looking for?   ....

2   thinks that Huck is a ghost?   ....

3   is Huck running away from?   ....

4   is Jim running away from?   ....

5   is Sarah Williams?   ....

6   is trying to get Huck's money?   ....

7   do people say killed Huck? .... or ....

8   are men going to look for on Jackson's Island?   ....

3.2 What more did you learn?

Look at this picture of Huck. How can he act more like a girl? Tell him what not to do. Use these words.

name	hat	walk	throw	catch

1   Don't ....
    ....!

2   ....
    ....!

3   ....
    ....!

4   ....
    ....!

5   ....
    ....!

.3 Language in use

Look at the sentences on the right. Then read the sentences below and make the two sentences into one, using an -*ing* verb form.

> I saw a man **sleeping** near it.
>
> There was something **lying** on the floor.

1 Huck saw a man. The man was wearing a coat over his head.
   Huck saw a man wearing a coat over his head

2 Jim heard the Widow. She was talking about him.

3 They saw a big house. It was coming down the river.

4 They found a man. He was lying on the floor.

5 There was a rat. It was looking for food.

6 Huck found Jim. Jim was sleeping in the tent.

.4 What happens next?

Discuss these questions and make notes about Huck and Jim's life on the river.

1 Why doesn't Huck want to be seen?

2 Why doesn't Jim want to be seen?

3 At what time of day do they travel?

4 What do they do as they travel?

5 What do they eat?

6 How do they keep dry?

7 What do they do if they can't see in front of them?

8 What will happen if their raft hits a boat?

Notes

CHAPTER 6

The Broken Steamboat

I thought, "What does Tom Sawyer do at times like this?
He doesn't run away." So I went inside.

In the daytime we hid in the woods near the river. One day, Jim made a tent on the raft. When it got too hot, we sat in the tent. We sat there when it rained, too.

At night, we traveled down the river on the raft. We didn't need to paddle— we just moved with the river. But we had to be careful. A lot of steamboats passed us at night and they couldn't see us. Steamboats are really big. If they hit a raft, the raft breaks to pieces. So when we saw one, we had to move away from it quickly.

Most nights we fished and talked. We passed a lot of towns on the river. Sometimes I went to a town in the canoe and bought food. Sometimes I "borrowed" a chicken. Pap always talked about "borrowing" things. But the Widow said, "That's just a nice name for stealing." Jim wasn't sure, so we

decided to make a list. Some things were OK to borrow. Other things weren't. We decided it was OK to borrow chickens, but not apples. I didn't like apples.

◆

One night, Jim and I were going down the river. We were about a hundred miles north of St. Louis. It was raining outside, so we were in the tent. I looked outside and saw something.

"Look, Jim!" I said. "There's an old broken steamboat!"

Part of the boat was under water, but most of it was still above water. The boat was on a big rock.

I said, "Let's paddle over to her."

But Jim didn't want to. He said, "It's too dangerous. Maybe somebody's living on it."

I told him, "Don't be stupid! The boat's going to **sink**. Nobody's living on it. Maybe we can borrow some things."

sink /sɪŋk/ (v) to go down under the water

So Jim agreed. "We'll have to be very careful," he said, "and we can't talk."

We paddled very quietly to the steamboat and got on it. It was too dark to see anything. Then I heard something. It was a man inside the steamboat.

He said, "No, please don't kill me. I won't tell anybody."

Then another person said, "That's a lie. You've said that before. This time we're going to kill you."

Jim ran to the raft. He wanted to get away from there. But I thought, "What does Tom Sawyer do at times like this? He doesn't run away." So I went inside.

I went in very quietly on my hands and knees. It was dark and I couldn't see anything. Then I came to a big room and I looked inside very carefully. There was a man on the floor and his hands and feet were tied. Then I saw two more men. One had a light, the other had a gun.

The man with the gun said, "I'm going to kill you now."

The man on the floor said, "No! No! Please don't! I won't tell anybody."

But the man with the gun laughed and said, "I'll make sure you don't tell anybody."

Then the man with the light said, "Put your gun away. We're not going to kill him. We'll leave him here. In a few hours this steamboat will sink, and he'll sink with it. I don't like to kill a man if I don't have to."

When I heard this, I ran outside. I found Jim and told him the story. I said, "We have to find their boat. If we take it away, they'll have to stay on the steamboat."

Jim didn't like the idea. He wanted to get away from there. But we found their boat on the other side of the steamboat. It was very dark and we almost didn't see it.

I was two feet away from the boat. Then just before I got in, a door opened. The man with the gun came out, but luckily he couldn't see us.

The man inside said, "Put that light out, Bill!"

The other man put a big bag in the boat. Then he got in and sat down. Then the other man got in. But they still didn't see me. Bill said, "Did you take the money from him?"

The other man answered, "No, I thought you took it. Let's go back and get it." And they both went back into the steamboat.

Jim and I moved very quickly. We jumped into their boat and pushed away from the steamboat. We didn't make any noise. The river was fast, so the boat moved along very quickly.

After a few minutes, we started to paddle, and soon we were safe. But then I started worrying about the men on the steamboat. I didn't want them to die.

So I told Jim, "The next time we see a light, we'll get help for them."

A short time later, I saw a small light in the window of a boat. I told Jim to meet me three miles down river. Then I got in the canoe.

When I reached the boat, the man was sleeping. I pushed his shoulder a few times and then I began to cry. The man woke up and said, "Don't cry, boy. What's the trouble?"

"It's Pap and Mom and my sister," I said. "There—on that steamboat. The one that hit the rock. We were crossing the river when the rain started. Our small boat sank and we all swam to the steamboat. Pap, Mom, and my sister are still on the boat. I swam here to get help."

"I'll get your family for you," the man said.

So I left him and ran back to my canoe. Then I went down the river to find Jim.

Soon I saw something coming down the river behind me. It was moving fast. It was the steamboat!

I paddled over to it and shouted, "Is anybody there?" But nobody answered. I thought, "If they're still on that steamboat, they're already dead."

Then I saw a second boat. In it was the man that I talked to. He was coming to save my family. I didn't want him to see me, so I paddled toward the side of the river.

When I found Jim I was very tired. We hid the canoe and the raft and sank the small boat. Then we went to sleep.

CHAPTER 7

Lost in the Fog

When I came up, I called for Jim. He didn't answer.
I looked for the raft, but it was in pieces.

The next day, Jim and I looked at the things from the men's boat. There were boots, clothes and a lot of books. I read some of the books to Jim. I read about kings and **duke**s, and Jim loved hearing those stories.

"I didn't know there were so many kings," he said. "How much money does a king get?"

"They get a thousand dollars a month if they want it," I told him. "Everything belongs to them."

Then he asked, "What do they do?"

"They don't do anything," I said. "Sometimes they go hunting. Sometimes they start a war."

Then I told him about King Louis the Sixteenth of France. "They cut off his head, and his son went to prison and died."

"That's terrible."

duke /duk/ (n) the title of a high-class European man whose oldest son will have the title after his death

"Some people say he escaped from prison. They say he came to America," I told him.

Jim asked, "What do kings do in America?"

I said, "They get a job with the police or something. Or maybe they teach French."

Jim said, "Huck, don't the French speak the same language as us?"

"No, they speak French," I told him.

He didn't believe me. "It's not right to speak different languages," he said.

So I said, "Jim, do cats talk the same way as we do?"

"No—no, they don't."

"And do dogs talk the same as we do?"

"No, I guess not."

"So," I said, "why is it different for the French? Can't they speak different from us?"

But Jim said, "A cat isn't a man, and a dog isn't a man. But the French, they're men. So they should talk like us."

I stopped then. Jim wasn't very smart. I knew this was too difficult for him.

That night, the river was covered in **fog**. We were about three days from Cairo, at the bottom of Illinois, and we couldn't see anything. It was too dangerous to be on the river. So I got in the canoe and pulled the raft to the side of the river. Then I tied the raft to a tree. But the tree was too small and the raft pulled it out. The raft, with Jim on it, started moving down the river.

For half a minute I was too worried to do anything. Then I got in my canoe. I paddled as quickly as I could. But the raft disappeared into the fog.

I called out to Jim. I heard a small shout far away and felt better. Jim was OK. But where was he? I shouted again. This time the answer came from behind me. I shouted again. Then the answer came from my right. This was bad news. I was turning around. Now I was lost, too.

I stopped paddling and listened. Sometimes Jim was in front of me, then he was behind me. Then I understood what was happening. I was near an island. Jim was on the other side of the island and he was moving faster than me. In the dark, it felt like I wasn't moving. But I was. Sometimes I hit the side of the river, and that turned my canoe around.

Soon I was in the middle of the river. I shouted again. Jim didn't answer. I tried again and again, but there was still no answer. I was feeling very tired and I wanted to sleep. I told myself to sleep for twenty minutes. Then I had to try to find Jim again.

I slept for more than twenty minutes. When I woke up, the stars were shining brightly. The sky was clear. So I went to find Jim. After a short time, I saw something in the river and paddled over to it. But when I got there, it was only an old piece of wood. I did that two more times before I found our raft.

When I got to it, Jim was sitting there asleep. I tied the canoe to the raft and got on the raft very quietly. I lay down.

Then I said, "Hello, Jim, have I been asleep?"

Jim said, "Huck, is that you? You're not dead? No, you're not. I was worried about you."

"What's the matter, Jim?" I said. "You're talking crazy. What are you talking about?"

Jim said, "You were lost in the fog last night. I called to you. I'm talking about that."

"That's really crazy," I said. "Jim, I know you love telling stories. But I was with you last night. I was here, asleep."

"Huck, are you saying there was no fog last night?"

"What fog?" I said.

fog /fɑɡ, fɔɡ/ (n) thick, cloudy air near the ground that is difficult to see through

"*The* fog. The fog that I got lost in. The fog that you were in. You shouted. I shouted. *That* fog!"

I said, "Jim, you were dreaming."

"Maybe I did dream it. But it was very real. I never had a dream as real as that before."

This was good fun. Jim really believed me. Then I told him—it was all a joke. He really was lost in the fog last night. That made him very angry. He said, "Why are you joking about that? I thought you were my friend. But a friend doesn't joke like that." Then he went into the tent.

I felt bad. It was fifteen minutes before he talked to me again. I was sorry about the joke.

We were very close to Cairo now, and Jim was very excited. He said, "When we get to Cairo I'll be a free man! They don't have slaves there."

Every time we passed a light, Jim jumped up and said: "Look! It's Cairo! I'm a free man!"

So I told Jim: "In the morning I'll ask somebody what town this is."

But that same night, two men came over in a boat. They had guns, too. One of the men said, "Who's over there?"

I said, "It's me and my raft."

"Are there any men on that raft?" he asked.

"Only one," I said.

"We're looking for five runaway slaves. Is the man on your raft white or black?" he asked.

"He's white," I answered.

"I think I'll check," said the man.

"Please do," I said. "It's Pap that's with me. Maybe you can help me take him into town. Pap is sick—and so is Mom and my sister, Mary Ann."

They agreed to help and started paddling over to us. Then I said, "It's good of you to help. I've talked to a lot of people, but nobody wanted to help."

"That wasn't very nice of them," said the man. "What's the problem with your pap?"

"It's the—it's the—it's nothing really."

Then they stopped paddling. "That's a lie, boy," the man said. "What *is* the problem with your pap? I want a true answer this time."

"I'll tell you, sir," I said. "But first come and help us get to town."

"Stop the boat, John," the man shouted. "You keep away, boy. If your pap is so sick, I don't want to come near him. Go about twenty miles down the river and you'll find a town. They can help you there." Then he said, "Do you have any money, boy?"

"No, sir," I said.

"Here's twenty dollars—that will pay for the doctor."

He put the money on a piece of wood and pushed it over to me.

I said, "Thank you very much, sir. I'll remember what you told me. Goodbye."

They both said, "Good luck."

When they were gone, I looked for Jim. He wasn't in the tent, so I shouted for him: "Jim, where are you?"

"Here I am," answered Jim. He was in the river. Only his head was above the water.

He got back on the raft and said, "I heard the men coming and I jumped into the river. I didn't want them to find me. I was going to swim away. But you tricked them, Huck. That was a good story. You saved my life. Nobody has ever helped me like that. You're the best friend that I have."

We talked about the money.

Jim said "I'm a free man, so I'll buy a ticket on a steamboat."

The next morning, we hid the raft and I went into town. I asked a man: "Is this town Cairo?"

"No," the man said, "You've gone past Cairo."

So I went back to the raft and told Jim. He wasn't a free man now. I felt really bad about going past it. But Jim said, "Huck, it's OK, I'll be free some day. Don't you worry."

◆

We slept all day, and the next night the fog came again. Jim and I were talking on the raft. We couldn't see anything and then we heard a steamboat. She was coming up the river but we couldn't see her.

The sound got louder. Then we saw her. She was coming straight for us! She was coming fast, too. Jim jumped off the raft and I jumped off, too. I swam straight down because I didn't want the boat to hit me. I was under water for a minute and a half. When I came up, I called for Jim. He didn't answer. I looked for the raft, but it was in pieces. The steamboat destroyed it.

I couldn't do anything about that, so I swam about two miles to the side of the river. When I climbed out, I looked for Jim again. I shouted for him, but he didn't answer. This time I was sure that he was dead.

4.1 Were you right?

Look back at Activity 3.4. Then complete these sentences.

Huck is running away from his .... and Jim wants to be a .... man. They travel on their raft at ...., staying away from .... If they can't see anything, they stop at the .... of the river. When it rains, they go inside their .... They talk and .... as they move down the river. They also buy or "borrow" ....

4.2 What more did you learn?

1 Put these in the right order, 1–6.

a ☐ Huck sees three men on the steamboat.

b ☐ Huck sees a broken steamboat.

c ☐ Huck tries to help the men on the steamboat.

d ☐ Jim and Huck take the thieves' boat.

e ☐ Huck and Jim paddle to the steamboat.

f ☐ The steamboat moves quickly down the river.

2 Look at the picture. Describe what happened. Use the words in the box.

noise fog steamboat raft destroy

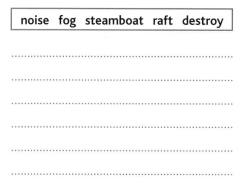

....

....

....

....

....

....

....

....

.3 Language in use

**Look at the sentences on the right.
Then complete the sentences below
with the verbs that are given.**

> We **were crossing** the river
> when the rain **started**.
>
> When I **reached** the boat, the
> man **was sleeping**.

1   It .... when Huck .... the broken
    steamboat. (rain, see)

2   When the man on the floor .... for his life, another man
    .... a gun. (ask, hold)

3   Huck .... in the canoe when the raft ....
    into the fog. (paddle, disappear)

4   When Huck .... the raft again, Jim ....
    (find, sleep)

5   The men .... for runaway slaves when they
    .... Huck on the raft. (look, see)

6   Jim and Huck .... on the raft when they
    .... a steamboat. (talk, hear)

.4 What happens next?

1   **In Chapter 7, who said these words? Write
    A or B. Who were they talking about?**

    A

    a   "Everything belongs to them."

        ☐ ....

    b   "They say he came to America."

        ☐ ....

    B

    c   "They should talk like us."

        ☐ ....

2   **Look at the picture on page 42. Circle the words
    that describe the two men.**

honest	smart	greedy	kind	stupid	rich	fair

CHAPTER 8

Huck Meets a Duke and a King

*Jim didn't know what to do. He had a king and a duke on his raft.
He didn't know what to do for a king.*

I was alone for a long time. I couldn't find Jim or my old canoe. I didn't know what to do. Then one day I was walking in the woods and I heard a voice: "Is that you, Huck?"

It was Jim. Nothing ever sounded so good. I ran to him, and he kissed me on the head. "I thought you were dead again," he said.

Jim had a new raft and he even had some food. We went down the river and talked. A raft is the best home, we agreed. You feel free on a raft. And the new raft was very comfortable, too.

◆

For two or three days we rested on the raft. The river was very big now. It was a mile and a half wide in places. We slept in the daytime and at night we went down the river. Some nights we didn't see anybody. We sat and looked at the stars.

"What are they made of?" I asked Jim. But Jim didn't know.

One day, I found a new canoe and I went to the side of the river. As I was paddling near the woods, two men ran toward me. I was worried. I thought it was their canoe.

Then one of the men shouted, "Help us! They're going to kill us!"

So it wasn't their canoe. I wasn't worried after that. I stopped and they jumped in. I paddled very quickly. One of the men was about seventy years old. He had no hair on his head but he had a gray beard. The other man was about thirty.

We got back to the raft and we all ate breakfast together.

"Who are you?" I asked.

The young man said, "I can tell you, but you won't believe me. I'm a duke. The Duke of Bridgewater."

Jim's eyes got really big. He couldn't believe it. A real duke—on his raft!

"That's wonderful," said the old man. "Then you and I have had similar lives."

We all looked at him. He said, "I'm the son of Louis the Sixteenth. My father was killed and I escaped to America. Now I live like this."

He looked at himself and began to cry. Jim didn't know what to do. He had a king and a duke on his raft. He didn't know what to do for a king.

"You should go down on one knee when you talk to me," the king told him. "And always feed me first at dinner."

So Jim and I started doing everything for the king. And we were on our knees all the time. He liked that, and the duke liked it, too.

I soon understood. These men weren't really a king and a duke. But Jim was very happy about it, so I didn't say anything.

They asked about Jim. "He's my slave," I told them. "We're going to my father's farm down river. People try to take Jim away from me. They think he's a runaway. So we have to travel at night."

The duke had an idea. He opened his bag and took out a piece of paper. On it he wrote "$200 REWARD." Then he wrote a description of Jim.

He said, "Now we can travel in the daytime. If somebody asks about him, we'll show them the piece of paper. We're taking him back to his farm. We should tie Jim's hands and feet. Then nobody will ask any questions."

We thought this was a good idea.

CHAPTER 9

The King's Success

Jim said to me, "They're a king and a duke, but they're not very honest."
But I told him about kings in books. Kings were always like that.

We traveled together for two days. The duke's idea was good. We traveled in the daytime and we didn't have any problems.

"I like to work in the theater," the king told us. "We can stop in the next town and do a play for them."

The duke made a sign for the play. It said:

STARTING TOMORROW!
For Three Nights Only
The Famous
DAVID GARRICK
and
EDMUND KEAN
From London
in
THE KING'S SUCCESS!!
Entrance 50 cents

Then at the bottom, in big letters, it said:

LADIES AND CHILDREN
NOT WELCOME

The next day, the king worked hard. He put up a big tent and inside the tent he made a stage. Then he was ready.

That night, a lot of people came. The duke took their money at the door and then he went onto the stage. He told the people about the play and the king. Then the show began.

Everyone was quiet. Then the king came on the stage. He was on his hands and knees, and he wasn't wearing any clothes! He was painted in many different colors.

The people laughed and laughed. I laughed, too. He looked so funny. Then the king left the stage. The people shouted, "More! More!" He had to do it again and again.

The duke came out and thanked everybody. They shouted, "Is that all?" Then they got angry and wanted to kill the duke and the king. But one man said, "Wait!

Listen, everybody. We were tricked by these two men, but we can't go home now. People will laugh at us. Tomorrow, tell everybody about this show. Tell them to see it tomorrow night. Then we'll trick *them*."

They all agreed to this. So the next night, there were even more people at the show and the same thing happened.

On the third night, the tent was full again. This time everybody from the town was there and they had eggs and old vegetables in their pockets. They planned to throw them at the king.

But the duke was a smart man. He gave a boy twenty-five cents to watch the entrance. He and I walked to the back of the tent. Then he said, "Run! Run as fast as you can!"

We ran all the way back to the raft.

When we got to the raft, we didn't wait for the king. We left as quickly as we could. I felt bad for the king. Those people were really angry.

Then I heard a voice from inside the tent. "How much money did we make?" it said.

It was the king! He was on the raft. He never even went into town.

The two men counted their money. They made $465 in three nights. Jim and I couldn't believe it. Jim said to me, "They're a king and a duke, but they're not very honest."

But I told him about kings in books. Kings were always like that.

CHAPTER 10

The **Funeral**

The king was very polite. He agreed to keep the money.
Then the king suggested that the girls come back to England with him.

We traveled all the next day. Jim was still tied up in the tent. That evening, he talked to the duke. "I don't like this. It hurts," he said.

"I'll think of another idea," said the duke.

He was a smart man and he soon had a new idea. He gave Jim some theater clothes that the king used. Then he painted Jim's face blue. He wrote a sign. It said, "This is a sick Arab, but he probably won't hurt you."

I was scared when I saw Jim. So it was a very good idea.

The king bought everybody new clothes with the money from "The King's Success." We still wore our old clothes on the raft. But when we went to town, we put on our new ones.

The duke wanted to make more money and he needed to think. He wanted to be alone. So I went to town with the king.

funeral /ˈfyunərəl/ (n) a service, for example in a church, for someone who has just died

We put on our new clothes and left in the canoe. We paddled toward the town. Near the town, we met a young man who was waiting for a steamboat to New Orleans. We stopped and offered him a ride to town.

Then he said, "Are you Mr. Wilks?"

"No," said the king, "my name is Blodgett, Alexander Blodgett. But tell me about Mr. Wilks. Is it an interesting story?"

So the young man told us about Mr. Wilks. His first name was Harvey and he came from England. His brother Peter lived here in the town, but he died the day before. The dead man left a lot of money to Harvey Wilks, but Mr. Wilks wasn't here yet.

Then the young man told us about the dead man's family. Peter Wilks had three daughters. The oldest daughter's name was Mary Jane. The young man talked about the dead man's farm and his money. And he told us about the dead man's other brother, William. William couldn't hear or speak. Nobody knew Harvey or William. That was because they lived together in England.

The king listened carefully to the story and he asked a lot of questions. He wanted to know about everybody and everything.

After a long time, we said goodbye to the young man, and he left on the steamboat. Then the king told me to go back to the raft. He said, "Go and get the duke. Tell him to come now. And tell him to bring the bags."

I got the duke and the bags. The duke didn't ask any questions. When we found the king, he said "hello." But he sounded strange because he was talking like an Englishman.

"Duke," he said, "my name is Harvey Wilks and you're my brother William. You can't hear or speak. Can you do that?"

"I can," the duke said.

We were about five miles from the town. When a steamboat came, we stopped it. We got on and went to the town.

45

There were a lot of people in town.

The king said, "Can someone please tell us where Mr. Peter Wilks lives?" He spoke like an Englishman.

One man said softly, "I'm sorry. I can't tell you where he lives. But I can tell you where he lived. He died yesterday evening. The funeral's tomorrow."

The king looked very sad. He turned to the duke and made some signs with his hands. The duke dropped his bags, and then he started to cry. I felt sick. I knew what they were planning. But I couldn't say anything, because I didn't want to get in trouble.

The people came around the king and the duke and said nice things. Then they took us to the dead man's house.

When we got to the house, the three daughters were waiting. Mary Jane kissed the king and the duke. She was very pretty. She had red hair and a very kind face. Then the king made a speech about his "poor dead brother." He remembered everything that the young man told him. He even remembered all the names.

Mary Jane left the room and came back with a letter from her dead father. She gave it to the king. There were $6,000 under the house, the letter said. So the king and the duke went to find it.

They found it easily. The duke counted the money, but there was only $5,585. Where were the other $415?

The king was worried. "They'll think we stole the $415."

But the duke had an idea. He said, "Let's put our money with it. That will make $6,000."

The king thought it was a great idea.

They went back up to the house and counted the money in front of everyone. Then the king gave another speech. He said, "This letter's from my brother. It says this money is for William and me. But William and I want to give this money to Mary Jane and her sisters. They'll need it."

The three sisters kissed the king and the duke. They were very happy. Only the doctor looked worried. He did not believe the king or the duke.

Next, Mary Jane said, "Uncle Harvey, you're very sweet. Thank you for the money, but please keep it for us. If we ever need it, we'll ask you."

The king was very polite. He agreed to keep the money. Then the king suggested that the girls come back to England with him. He said, "We can sell the house and the slaves and we'll all go to England tomorrow."

Everybody thought it was a good idea. They all went to bed thinking about it.

The king hid the money under his bed and went to sleep. I couldn't sleep because I felt bad for Mary Jane and her sisters. I couldn't tell them about the king and the duke.

But then I had an idea. While the king was asleep, I took the money. I went downstairs and hid it. When I was going back to bed, I saw Mary Jane. She was in her bedroom crying. I felt really bad for her, so I decided to tell her about the king and the duke. I went into her room and said, "Miss Mary Jane, I don't like to see people cry." Then I said, "Miss Mary Jane, those uncles of yours aren't really your uncles. They're bad men—they only want to steal your money."

She was very angry. "What can I do?" she asked.

"You should visit some friends for a few days. Then, when the men have gone, you can call the police."

Mary Jane agreed to leave with her sisters after the funeral. Then I sat down and wrote a letter. I wrote:

Miss Mary Jane,
Your money is with your dead father. I saw you sitting with him last night and you were crying. I was hiding behind the door. I put the money in later.

I gave her the letter and said, "Don't read this until those two men have gone."

When the king couldn't find the money, he was very angry. "Did you steal it?" he asked me.

"Of course not," I said, and he believed me.

That morning, he sold the slaves and the house. He didn't get much money for them, but he didn't worry about that. He was still angry that somebody stole his $6,000. A little money was better than no money. Now they could get away from this town.

In the afternoon, we all went to the funeral. The church was full and everyone sat quietly. We sang, and then the king said some nice words. A lot of people cried. Then we all went back to the house.

"We have to leave now," the king told Mary Jane.

Mary Jane said, "We have to visit some friends before we go with you to England. We'll meet you later."

So the king, the duke, and I went to the river and waited for the steamboat. When it came, two men got off. One of them said, "I'm Peter Wilks's brother, Harvey. This is my brother, William." He spoke like a *real* Englishman.

Things went crazy after that. People asked the men a lot of questions, and they looked angrily at the king and the duke. Everybody was watching them and they forgot about me. So I walked away slowly and quietly. Then I started to run. I ran all the way to the river.

When I got to the raft, I shouted for Jim. He came out of the tent. I was very scared when I saw him. I forgot that he was dressed as a crazy Arab.

I said, "We've got to go right now!"

Then I heard voices. It was the king and the duke. I almost cried—I never wanted to see them again. But they got on the raft and we all went down the river.

5.1 Were you right?

Look back at Activity 4.4, 2. Then read these sentences. Are they true (T) or not true (NT)?

1 The king wants Huck and Jim to do everything for him. ....

2 He and his friend are a real king and duke. ....

3 They put on an excellent show in the town. ....

4 They make a lot of money from their show. ....

5 They try to trick the Wilks family. ....

6 They sell the Wilks's house and slaves. ....

7 They steal $6,000 from the Wilks family. ....

8 The Wilks don't find out about their tricks. ....

5.2 What more did you learn?

Complete the sentences with words from boxes A and B.

A Huck Jim Mary Jane The people in the town	**B** pain afraid angry worried happy sad

1 ....Jim..................... was .... that a king and a duke joined them on the raft.

2 .... were .... when they saw the king and the duke's show.

3 .... was in .... because his hands and feet were tied.

4 .... was .... because her father was dead.

5 .... was .... about the king and the duke's plan to get the Wilks's money.

6 .... was .... when he saw Jim again in Arab clothes.

3 Language in use

Look at the sentences on the right.
Then complete each of the sentences
below with a word from the box.

> "Can someone please tell us
> **where** Mr. Peter Wilks lives?"
>
> I knew **what** they were planning.

why	where	what	who	how

1 Huck asked Jim .... the stars were made of.

2 Huck asked the two men .... they were.

3 The king and the duke asked .... Jim was traveling with Huck.

4 The king and the duke knew .... they could get money from people.

5 The king wanted to know .... everybody in the Wilks family was.

6 A man told the king .... the Wilks family lived.

7 Mary Jane asked Huck .... she could do about the king and the duke.

8 Huck told Mary Jane .... the money was hidden. .

4 What happens next?

Look at the picture and discuss these questions. Make notes.

1 What has happened to Jim?

2 Why?

3 How?

4 What is going to happen to him?

Notes

CHAPTER 11

Where's Jim?

"It's Jim. He's a prisoner. I'm going to help him escape."
"That sounds fun," Tom said. "I'll help."

For days and days we didn't stop at any towns. We were down south in warm weather now, and a very long way from home. The king and the duke fought all the time. They were very angry about losing their money. But they needed a new idea, so they decided to work together again.

The next morning, we stopped near a town and hid the raft in the tall grass.

"I'm going into town," the king said to the duke and me. "I'll take our last few dollars. Wait until twelve o'clock. Then come and find me."

We waited, and at twelve o'clock the duke and I went to town. Jim stayed on the raft.

We found the king, but he didn't have any money. The duke got very angry and started shouting at the king. The king started to shout back. While they were fighting, I ran back to the raft. I shouted, "Jim come out! Let's go!"

But Jim didn't answer. I shouted and shouted, but I couldn't find him.

Soon I saw a boy walking in the woods. I asked, "Have you seen an old black man around here?" I described him, and his clothes.

"Yes, I saw him," said the boy. "He's a slave, and he's run away from his owner. He's at Mr. Phelps's farm, two miles from here. Are you looking for him?"

"No," I said quickly. "I saw him in the woods. He scared me, so I hid."

"You're safe now," he said. "A stranger found him. He told Mr. Phelps about him and Mr. Phelps gave him forty dollars for the information. Now the slave's a prisoner at his farm. His owner will give a $200 reward to the person who finds him. I saw the sign."

I remembered the duke's "$200 REWARD" sign and felt sorry for Jim. Now he was in big trouble. I wanted to help him. I tried to think of an idea, but I couldn't. I remembered all the things that Jim and I did. I remembered all the times that he helped me. I was his best friend. I was his *only* friend. I decided to steal Jim away from Mr. Phelps.

First, I hid the raft on an island down river. I slept there that night and the next morning I took the canoe to the riverside. I filled it with rocks and sank it. Then I started walking up the road.

The Phelpses' farm was very small. I walked to the back of the house. Suddenly, a woman ran out. She was smiling.

She said, "It's you, at last! We've waited for you for three days. Come and give your Aunt Sally a kiss." She took me inside and said, "Children, this is your cousin Tom. Say hello."

They said "hello" to me. I didn't know what to do. She offered me some breakfast but I wasn't hungry. She asked a lot of questions about my boat trip, and then she asked, "And where are your bags?"

"I left them in town," I told her. "They were very heavy."

Then she asked, "So, how is my sister? Tell me all about her."

I didn't know what to say. I opened my mouth to tell her my real name, but she stopped me. She said, "Here comes my husband. He was looking for you in town. Let's play a trick on him. Hide behind this chair."

Her husband came in. "He hasn't come," he told his wife. "I'm very worried about him." Then he turned and looked out the window.

Aunt Sally pulled me up so I was standing behind the bed. The man turned back from the window.

He looked at me. "Who's that?"

She said, "It's *Tom Sawyer*!"

I couldn't believe it! I almost laughed when I heard it. But I didn't have time. The old man shook my hand, and the woman laughed and cried. And they both asked a lot of questions about Tom's family.

I was so happy. I knew everything about Tom's family, so we talked for a long time.

But then I heard a steamboat. Maybe the *real* Tom was on it. So I said, "I have to go to town. I want to get my bags. Can I take your **wagon**?"

"Of course," the old man said.

When I wasn't far from town, I saw a wagon. A boy was driving it. It was Tom! I stopped and waited. When he got to me, he stopped his wagon. His eyes were big and his mouth was open. He said, "Huck Finn, I never hurt you. Why have you come to scare me? What do you want?"

I said, "I haven't come back. I never went!"

"Aren't you a ghost?"

"No," I said.

"Weren't you killed?"

"No, I wasn't."

I told him about my adventures. He thought about the problem of the Phelpses and had an idea. He said, "Don't tell Aunt Sally or Uncle Silas about me. You're still Tom Sawyer. Take your bags in my wagon and go back to the farm. I'll be there soon."

wagon /ˈwægən/ (n) a strong vehicle with four wheels, usually pulled by horses

I agreed. "But there's one more thing," I said. "It's Jim. He's a prisoner. I'm going to help him escape."

"That sounds fun," Tom said. "I'll help."

I couldn't believe that Tom wanted to help. It was illegal to help a runaway slave. I got Jim into this trouble, so I *had* to help. But I didn't know why Tom wanted to help.

"You're joking!" I said.

"I'm not joking," said Tom.

"OK," I said, "but if anybody talks about a runaway slave, you don't know anything about it."

So I went back to the farm. Tom came half an hour later.

When Aunt Sally saw Tom, she said, "Who's that coming up the road?"

Uncle Silas went out to meet him.

Tom said, "Are you Mr. Nichols?"

Uncle Silas answered, "No, my boy, I'm not. Mr. Nichols lives three miles up the road. But come in and sit down. You can have dinner with us. After dinner, I'll take you to the Nicholses' place in my wagon."

"That's OK, sir," said Tom, "I can walk. It won't take long."

"No, no, I'll take you," answered Uncle Silas.

So Tom agreed and thanked the Phelpses. He walked in the house and greeted everybody. He said, "My name's William Thompson, from Hicksville, Ohio." Then he walked over to Aunt Sally and kissed her on the mouth.

She said, "What are you doing?"

Tom said, "I'm surprised at you, ma'am."

"You're surprised at me? *I'm* surprised at *you*! Why did you kiss me?"

"I thought you'd like it," said Tom.

"What? Why did you think I'd like it, you stupid boy?" shouted Aunt Sally.

"I'm sorry," said Tom, "I won't do it again—until you ask me to."

"Until I ask you to! Boy, you're crazy," cried Aunt Sally.

"I don't understand," said Tom. "I thought you'd like it. But—" Then he stopped. He looked at Uncle Silas and said, "Didn't *you* think she'd like a kiss from me, sir?"

"No, I-I—no I don't believe I did," said Uncle Silas.

Then Tom looked at me and said, "Tom, didn't you think Aunt Sally liked Sid Sawyer?"

Then Aunt Sally jumped up and said, "Sid Sawyer! I can't believe it!"

Then she ran across the room and tried to kiss him. But he pushed her away and said, "No, not until you ask me to kiss you."

CHAPTER 12

Escape Plans

"But I don't want rats in here," said Jim.
But Tom told him, "You have to have rats. You're in prison."

So Tom was Sid, and everybody was happy. They all came and kissed him again and again.

We had dinner and talked all afternoon. Tom and I listened hard, but nobody said anything about Jim.

That night, Tom and I decided to go to town.

"I've seen signs for a show," Tom said. "It's called 'The King's Success.'"

I told him about the king and the duke.

"Then we have to go," he said.

So we climbed out our bedroom window and walked to town.

There was a lot of noise in town, so we went to look. It wasn't a fight—it was the king and the duke. People were driving them out of town. They knew about their show from Uncle Silas. *He* knew about it from Jim. The king and the duke were in trouble.

We started walking back home and we talked about Jim. We didn't know where he was. But there was a small cabin near the house.

Tom said, "Maybe he's in there. The door's locked, and a slave took some food there this evening."

We both sat down. We had to think of a plan. How could we help Jim to escape?

After some time, I said, "We can steal the key and take Jim to the canoe. Then we can paddle across the river. On the other side he'll be free. What do you think, Tom? Will it work?"

"Of course it'll work," said Tom, "but it's too easy. I read about this in a book. Escaping takes a long time. Your plan's too quick."

When we got back to the farm, we looked at the cabin.

Tom said, "There's only one way. We'll have to **dig** a hole."

"That's easy," I said. I went to get some big tools.

But when Tom saw them, he said, "We can't use those tools. We have to use knives. That's what they use in books. I've read a lot of escape stories. They always use knives."

"That'll take a week—maybe two," I said. "It's a stupid idea."

But Tom said, "I've never read about any other way of digging. And I've read all the books. It's the right way."

dig /dɪg/ (v) to move earth with a tool or your hands to make a hole in the ground

So we started digging. We only dug two inches before midnight. Our hands hurt and we were very tired.

Then Tom said, "It isn't going to work, Huck. We'll have to use the big tools."

I said, "At last! Tom, you get smarter and smarter all the time."

Then we stopped for the night.

The next day, Tom said, "We need an old shirt for Jim."

"What does Jim need an old shirt for?" I asked.

"He can write messages on the shirt," Tom said.

I said, "But, Tom, Jim can't write."

"That's not important," said Tom. "We have to do it. And we need a big knife, too."

"What for?" I asked.

"Huck, you *are* stupid. Jim's in prison, so his feet are tied. We have to cut off his feet to free him. So we need a big knife."

"But why don't we just untie him?" I said. "How can he run away if he has no feet?"

Tom agreed that it was difficult to run with no feet. So I didn't have to get a big knife.

That night, we finished digging the hole. Jim was very glad to see us. He almost started to cry. We gave him the shirt.

Then Tom said, "Do you have any rats in here, Jim?"

Jim said, "No, this is a clean cabin."

So Tom said, "Don't worry, we'll get you some."

"But I don't want rats in here," said Jim.

But Tom told him, "You have to have rats. You're in prison. Prisons always have rats."

Jim didn't understand. But all white people were crazy, so he agreed.

Tom said, "Good! I'll bring some rats tomorrow."

We told Jim about our escape plans. We weren't ready yet. He had to wait until tomorrow—or maybe the next day. Then we said goodnight.

We went back to the house and went to bed.

6.1 Were you right?

Find the correct endings to the sentences.

1	Huck is told that Jim ...	is Sid Sawyer.
2	Huck learns that Mrs. Phelps ...	is Tom Sawyer.
3	Mrs. Phelps thinks that Huck ...	is alone in a locked cabin.
4	At first Tom says that he ...	is a prisoner on a farm.
5	Later, he says that he ...	is from Ohio.
6	All this time, Jim ...	is Tom Sawyer's aunt.

6.2 What more did you learn?

Who is speaking? Write A–D. What is happening? Write a–f.

 A  B  C 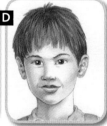 D

a The boys have finished digging a hole.

b She was kissed.

c Two wagons meet on the road.

d The boys are digging a hole.

e The boys are worried that Jim can't move.

f There is nobody on the raft.

> Jim, come out! Let's go!

1 [A] [f]

> You get smarter and smarter all the time.

4 ☐ ☐

> Aren't you a ghost?

2 ☐ ☐

> We have to cut off his feet to free him.

5 ☐ ☐

> Why did you think I'd like it, you stupid boy?!

3 ☐ ☐

> But I don't want rats in here.

6 ☐ ☐

.3 Language in use

Look at the sentences on the right. Then complete the sentences below with present perfect verb forms.

> **Have** you **seen** an old black man around here?
>
> He**'s run** away from his owner.

1 Aunt Sally said, "We' .... for you for three days." (wait)

2 Mr. Phelps said, "He .... I'm very worried about him." (not come)

3 Tom asked, "Why .... you .... to scare me?" (come)

4 Huck said, "I .... back." (not come)

5 Tom said, "I' .... signs for a show." (see)

6 Tom said, "I' .... a lot of escape stories." (read)

.4 What happens next?

How do you think the story will end? Which of these pictures show what will happen?

CHAPTER 13

Prison Life

One man said, "Who's that? Answer or I'll shoot!"
We didn't answer. We ran!

"I've looked everywhere, but I can't find your other shirt." Aunt Sally was hot, red, and angry at breakfast.

For a minute I felt scared, and Tom turned a little blue.

"I saw it outside yesterday," said Aunt Sally. "You'll have to wear a red one until I can make a new one. What have you done with it?"

"I don't know. I can't understand it," said Uncle Silas.

Tom and I finished breakfast quickly. Then we went outside.

We had to do a lot of things that day. First, we had to catch some rats for Jim. Then Tom had another idea. He said, "In prison, people always write on the wall. They write something each day. Jim has to do that." He thought for a

minute, and then he said, "The cabin has wooden walls. But prisons have stone walls, not wooden ones. We need to find a big rock so Jim can write on that."

We looked everywhere for a big rock and in the afternoon we found one. But it was too heavy for us, so we waited until night. Then we untied Jim and took him with us to the rock.

Jim said, "I can get out of this cabin. So why don't we run away?"

"You have to write on the stone first," Tom told him. "Then you can escape."

With Jim's help, we carried the rock and put it in Jim's cabin. Now Jim had to write on it every day.

So Jim had to stay in prison another day. We gave him the rats and said goodnight.

Jim said, "I really don't like rats."

"You have to have them," Tom told him.

Jim said, "I hope I get out of here. I never want to go to prison again."

We went back to the house, but we didn't go to bed.

Tom said, "Everything's ready. Now we only need the letter."

"What letter?" I said.

"We have to tell people that something's going to happen."

"Why do you want to do that? Don't tell them about the escape! They'll catch him again!"

But Tom said, "We have to. The books always say that. We have to write a letter. They have to know because they have to try and stop us. Or it'll be too easy."

So we wrote the letter. It was a very good letter. It said:

Be careful. You're in trouble. There is a gang of robbers coming. They want to steal your slave from prison. They're coming tonight. Don't do anything. You will be safe in your house. They only want your slave.

A friend

We thought it was a fine letter. Tom climbed out the window and put it under the front door. Then he came back and we went to sleep. Everything was ready.

We felt really good in the morning. After breakfast we took the canoe and went fishing. We got the raft ready for the escape.

We arrived home really late. Aunt Sally was worried about us and after supper she sent us straight to bed. But Tom and I needed some food for the escape, so I went down to the kitchen. I was taking some bread and butter when suddenly Aunt Sally came in. I put the bread on the table and the butter under my hat.

Aunt Sally shouted at me. "What are you doing?" she said.

"I want a drink of water," I answered.

Aunt Sally wasn't happy. She took my arm and pulled me into the living-room. There, I saw fifteen or twenty farmers and every man had a gun.

Aunt Sally said, "A gang of robbers are coming tonight, so go to bed. And stay away from the window or you'll get hurt!"

Suddenly, she stopped talking. She looked at me and pulled off my hat. She started to laugh. Then everybody in the room started to laugh. The butter under my hat was too hot and it was running down my head. Aunt Sally got me some food and sent me to bed.

I ran upstairs and told Tom about the men with guns. I was really scared but Tom was excited. "This will be the best escape in history!" he said.

"Hurry!" I said.

So we climbed out our window and went to the cabin. We went under it, through our hole, and got Jim. Then we climbed out through the hole. Everything was going well.

We walked silently toward the river, but then Tom's jeans caught on a tree. When he pulled them free, it made a lot of noise.

Somebody shouted, "Who's that?"

Tom got really excited and shouted, "YAHOOO!!"

Just then the front door of the house opened. All the men came running out with their guns.

One man said, "Who's that? Answer or I'll shoot!"

We didn't answer. We ran! We ran as fast as we could across the yard toward the woods. Then we heard "bang, bang, bang!" We didn't stop.

Somebody said, "There they are! They're running to the river!"

We got to the river and found my canoe. We pushed it away. It was very dark, so the men couldn't see us on the river. We paddled as fast as we could.

When we got to the island and the raft, I said, "Jim, now you're a free man. You'll never be a slave again."

CHAPTER 14

Yours, Huck Finn

Aunt Sally ran, crying, to Tom.
She said, "He's dead! He's dead! I know he's dead!"

We were all as happy as we could be. Jim was glad to be free. I was glad that I helped Jim. Tom was the gladdest of all of us because he was shot in the leg!

Jim and I looked at Tom's leg. We weren't so happy then. His leg was hurting, and there was a lot of blood. So we put him in the tent and then we found an old shirt and tied it around Tom's leg. But I told Jim, "Tom needs a doctor."

Jim agreed. He said, "I'm a free man now. Maybe they'll catch me again but I don't want my friend to die."

So I went to find a doctor. Tom didn't like the idea, but I had to go. Jim promised to hide in the woods when the doctor came.

The doctor was a very nice, kind old man.

"My brother's hurt," I told him. "We were hunting and he had an accident. He was shot in the leg."

The doctor came with me to the river. When he saw the canoe, he stopped. "It doesn't look very strong," he said.

"It's a good canoe," I said.

"I'll find a bigger one."

"Then you need to go across the river to that island. I'll be there soon, with my brother."

"Fine, I'll see you there."

I was very tired, so I found a quiet place. I went to sleep.

When I woke up, it was late. I ran to the doctor's house, but he wasn't there.

"He's helping a boy who was shot," his wife explained.

I decided to go back to Tom and Jim, and I ran back to the canoe. As I turned a corner, I met Uncle Silas!

"Tom, what are you doing here? Where have you been? Your Aunt Sally's been worried about you!"

"Sid and I went to look for the slave," I told him. "Sid will be back soon."

"Come to the house with me now," he said.

I went back to the house. Aunt Sally was really glad to see me. She laughed and cried and then she kissed me.

"I must go and find Sid," I told her.

"No, don't do that. Stay here," Aunt Sally said.

She was worried about him. I really wanted to go, but I decided to stay at the house. I didn't want to give Aunt Sally more trouble.

I slept badly that night because I was thinking about Tom.

At breakfast, Aunt Sally was still very worried about Sid. Then she stopped talking when she saw something outside. It was Tom Sawyer! A young man was carrying him and the old doctor was with him, too. And then I saw Jim. His hands were tied behind him.

Aunt Sally ran, crying, to Tom. She said, "He's dead! He's dead! I know he's dead!"

Tom turned his head and he said something. I didn't hear what he said.

Aunt Sally shouted, "He's alive! He's alive!" And she started to cry again.

I went to see Tom. But I also listened to the men talking. I was worried about Jim and I didn't want them to hurt him. Some of the men wanted to kill Jim. Some men hit him a few times on the head. But Jim never said anything.

The old doctor said, "Don't hurt him. He's not a bad man. He helped me to save the boy's life. And he didn't fight us when we tied his hands."

So the men stopped hitting Jim. Then they locked him in the cabin again.

Tom slept all that day. Aunt Sally sat with him all night, too. In the morning, I went into his room. Aunt Sally was still there. Tom was sleeping quietly.

I waited, and then he opened his eyes. "Hello," he said. "Why am I home? Where's the raft? Where's Jim?"

"Everything's fine," I said.

"Good," he said. "Did you tell Aunt Sally?"

"Tell me what, Sid?"

"About the escape. It was great fun!"

Aunt Sally thought Tom was crazy. But I told her nearly everything.

She got angry. Then she said, "I hope you enjoyed it. But that slave's in big trouble now."

Tom looked at me. He said, "You said, 'Everything's fine.' Isn't Jim still free?"

"*Him?*" said Aunt Sally. "No. he isn't. He's locked in the cabin again."

Tom sat up. He looked very angry. He shouted, "You can't keep him! He's a free man!"

"What do you mean, Sid? Are you crazy?" said Aunt Sally.

"No, I'm not," said Tom. "He was the Widow Douglas's slave. The Widow died two months ago. Before she died, she freed him. He's not a slave now!"

"Then why did you and Tom help him to escape?"

"We wanted an adventure," said Tom. "And it was a great adventure, too."

Then Tom's eyes opened wide. He was looking at the door. "Aunt Polly!" he said.

Tom lived with his Aunt Polly in St. Petersburg. But that was eleven hundred miles away. What was she doing here? Now we were in real trouble.

Aunt Sally jumped up to kiss Aunt Polly. Tom looked away. I hid under the bed.

Aunt Polly pushed Aunt Sally away and said, "What's the matter with you, Tom?"

"That's not Tom," said Aunt Sally, "That's Sid. Tom is—Tom is—Where *is* Tom? He was here a minute ago!"

Aunt Polly said, "He's under the bed. But he's not Tom. He's Huck Finn. Come out from under the bed, Huck Finn!"

So I came out. I was really scared. Aunt Sally didn't understand until Aunt Polly told her about me. Then I told my story.

"I'm sorry, Mrs. Phelps," I said.

"You can still call me Aunt Sally," she said.

Then Aunt Polly said, "Tom's right. The Widow *is* dead and Jim's a free man. Thank you for your letter, Sally. You wrote about Tom and Sid, but Sid was at home with me. I knew there was trouble. 'What's Tom doing this time?' I asked myself. So I got on the next steamboat."

Then we went out and got Jim. He was very happy to see us. And he was happier when he heard the news. He was a free man! But he felt bad about the Widow.

Tom gave Jim forty dollars because he was a good prisoner. Jim looked at me. He said, "Didn't I tell you, Huck? 'I have hairy arms. That means I'm going to be rich.' Now I have forty dollars and I *am* rich!"

"Let's run away to town," Tom said. "We'll buy some warm clothes and then we'll go on a new adventure."

But I didn't have any money for new clothes. I said, "My money was with the Judge. Pap probably has it now."

"Don't worry about your pap," Jim said. "He doesn't have your money and he isn't coming back."

"How do you know?" I asked, but he didn't tell me.

I asked again and again. I really wanted to know.

At last he said, "Remember that house that we found? The one on the river? There was a dead man in the house. I told you not to look at him. Huck, that dead man was your pap. So you can get your money when you want it."

◆

Tom's almost well now, so that's the end of the story. I'm glad it's finished. Writing's difficult. I'm never going to write another book. I'm going to leave soon because Aunt Sally wants to teach me to be polite. But I've done that before, and I didn't like it.

The End

Yours,

Huck Finn

1 Discuss, in small groups, what Huck should do next, in your opinion. Should he do any of these?

Should he live alone or with Jim?

Should he save his money or spend it?

Should he live inside or in the woods?

Should he see Tom again or not?

Should he work or go to school?

Should he try to make more friends or not?

2 Discuss these questions with another student and make notes below. Then discuss the same questions with the class.

a Why did Mark Twain decide to make Huck Finn the storyteller?

b How is Huck Finn different from Tom Sawyer? How are they similar?

c How are Tom and Huck's lives different from the lives of boys today?

d Who did you like most in the book? Who did you like least? Why?

e Which was your favorite part of the story? Why?

f Were you surprised by the lifestyles of anyone in the book? Whose?

Notes

Work in pairs. This book is Huck's story. But imagine that it is Jim's story. Of course, Jim can't read or write.

Student A | You are Jim. Think of something that happened in the story. Where were you? What happened? What did you see? How did you feel? What happened next? Tell your friend.

Student B | You are Jim's friend. Listen to his story and write it for him. Ask him to repeat information if necessary. Ask questions if you need more information. When you have finished, give the story a title.

1 Work in a small group with other students. Choose a part of the story when Huck was enjoying life on the Mississippi River. Discuss these questions.

a   What was enjoyable about life on the river?

b   What would you enjoy doing on or near a big river?

2 Use books or the Internet to find out more about the Mississippi River. What would you like to know? Then write the names of the cities and states on the map.

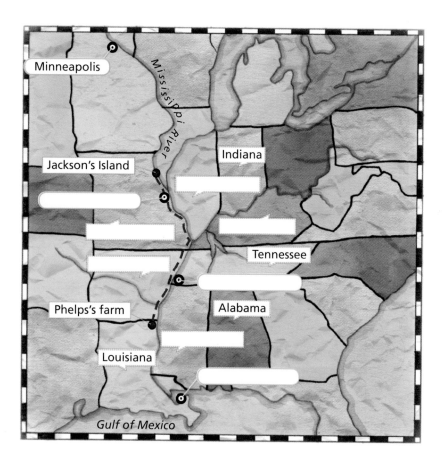

Imagine that, as a group, you have started a new company. The company organizes "Huckleberry Finn" vacations on the Mississippi River. Discuss possible vacations for visitors to the area.

| Student A | You think that visitors should sleep in tents or in cabins. They can fish, make a fire, and then cook their food on the fire. |

| Student B | You think that visitors should stay in a big hotel next to the Mississippi River. They will be able to swim in a nice pool and eat in a good restaurant. |

| Student C | You think that visitors should stay on a steamboat and travel down the river on it. In different places on the trip, actors can act parts of the story. |

| Other students | Listen to these opinions and give yours. Then decide which vacation is best. You must all agree. |

Now discuss which of these vacation activities will be most important to your visitors. Number them, 1–10. Then decide how many you will offer. You must all agree.

☐ Swimming

☐ Fishing

☐ Watching actors show parts of a story

☐ Hunting

☐ Horse riding

☐ Open fires

☐ Games

☐ Walks next to the river

☐ Canoeing

☐ Steamboat rides

5 **How are you going to sell "Huckleberry Finn Vacations" to customers? Look at the advertisement below. Then discuss these questions and plan or write your own advertisement.**

a How will you try to reach customers? Will you use television, radio, newspapers, magazines, or the Internet?

b What do you want to tell people about your vacations? What is the best way of doing that?

IS MODERN LIFE TOO FAST?
TAKE A BREAK, LIKE HUCK FINN, BY THE MISSISSIPPI RIVER.

HUCKLEBERRY FINN VACATIONS